GEORGIA
BULLDOGS

BY JEFF SEIDEL

SportsZone

An Imprint of Abdo Publishing
abdopublishing.com

abdopublishing.com

Published by Abdo Publishing, a division of ABDO, PO Box 398166, Minneapolis, Minnesota 55439.
Copyright © 2019 by Abdo Consulting Group, Inc. International copyrights reserved in all countries.
No part of this book may be reproduced in any form without written permission from the publisher.
SportsZone™ is a trademark and logo of Abdo Publishing.

Printed in the United States of America, North Mankato, Minnesota
022018
092018

Cover Photo: David Goldman/AP Images
Interior Photos: David Goldman/AP Images, 1; Focus on Sport/Getty Images, 4–5; Andy Hayt/Sports
Illustrated/Getty Images, 8; Gene Blythe/AP Images, 11; Sean Pavone/Shutterstock Images, 12–13;
University of Georgia/Collegiate Images/Getty Images, 15, 22, 42 (top); AP Images, 16, 18–19, 43 (top
right); Bettmann/Getty Images, 21, 43 (top left); Fred Kaufman/AP Images, 24–25; Todd Kirkland/Icon
Sportswire/AP Images, 26; Mario Suriani/AP Images, 29, 42 (bottom); Nick Arroyo/The Atlanta Journal-
Constitution/AP Images, 30–31; Scott Audette/AP Images, 33; John Bazemore/AP Images, 34; Rob Carr/
AP Images, 36–37, 43 (bottom left); Al Messerschmidt/Getty Images Sport/Getty Images, 39; Justin
Cooper/Cal Sport Media/AP Images, 41, 43 (bottom right)

Editor: Patrick Donnelly
Series Designer: Craig Hinton

Library of Congress Control Number: 2017962091

Publisher's Cataloging-in-Publication Data

Names: Seidel, Jeff, author.
Title: Georgia Bulldogs / by Jeff Seidel.
Description: Minneapolis, Minnesota : Abdo Publishing, 2019. | Series: Inside college football | Includes
    online resources and index.
Identifiers: ISBN 9781532114571 (lib.bdg.) | ISBN 9781532154409 (ebook)
Subjects: LCSH: American football--Juvenile literature. | College sports--United States--History-
    -Juvenile literature. | University of Georgia. Bulldogs (Football team)--Juvenile literature. |
    Football--Records--United States--Juvenile literature.
Classification: DDC 796.332630--dc23

TABLE OF CONTENTS

1 A PERFECT SEASON 4

2 THE EARLY DAYS 12

3 SOUTHERN CHAMPIONS 18

4 DOOLEY CHANGES
EVERYTHING 24

5 LEAN YEARS 30

6 LOOKING FOR A WINNER 36

TIMELINE 42

QUICK STATS 44

QUOTES & ANECDOTES 45

GLOSSARY 46

MORE INFORMATION 47

ONLINE RESOURCES 47

INDEX 48

ABOUT THE AUTHOR 48

Running back Herschel Walker tore up the SEC as a freshman in 1980.

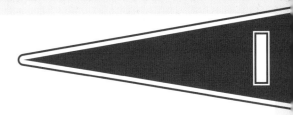

A PERFECT SEASON

THE COLLEGE FOOTBALL EXPERTS THOUGHT THE UNIVERSITY OF GEORGIA WOULD HAVE AN IMPROVED TEAM IN 1980. THE BULLDOGS WERE RANKED NO. 16 IN THE ASSOCIATED PRESS PRESEASON POLL. BUT NO ONE COULD HAVE PREDICTED THE IMPACT THAT A NEW FACE IN ATHENS, GEORGIA, WOULD HAVE ON THE COLLEGE FOOTBALL WORLD THAT YEAR.

The Bulldogs had generally been a strong team throughout coach Vince Dooley's time at Georgia. But in 1979, the offense was inconsistent and the team stumbled to a 6–5 record. For the second time in three years, the Bulldogs were not invited to a bowl game.

Looking to change its fortunes, Georgia began the 1980 season with a game at Southeastern Conference (SEC) rival Tennessee. The Georgia coaches used a few different running backs in the first half. One was a freshman from Wrightsville, Georgia, named Herschel Walker. None of them had much success as Tennessee took a 9–0 lead into halftime.

Then the Georgia coaches made a decision that changed the future of the program. Dooley wasn't known for giving playing time to freshmen. But he decided to end the running back rotation and give Walker the ball in the second half.

Tennessee extended its lead to 15–2. Then Walker took over. First he made one of the most famous plays in Georgia history. Walker took a handoff, cut through a huge hole on the left side of the line, and built up a head of steam. Tennessee safety Bill Bates tried to make a one-on-one tackle just inside the 10-yard line. But Walker simply ran over Bates on his path to the end zone.

That 16-yard touchdown run cut the Volunteers' lead to 15–9. Walker then struck again, scoring from 9 yards out. Rex Robinson's extra point gave the Bulldogs a one-point lead, and Georgia held on for a 16–15 victory.

The Bulldogs moved up to No. 12 in the national poll after that win, and they kept climbing. Behind Walker's powerful running, the Bulldogs won the next five games to push their record to 6–0 and found themselves ranked fifth in the country. A 27–0 victory at Kentucky bumped Georgia to No. 4. The next week, a 13–10 win over No. 14 South Carolina left the Bulldogs ranked No. 2, behind only Notre Dame.

The next week, 20th-ranked Florida provided the stiffest test yet. Walker scored on a 72-yard run in the first quarter, part of a 238-yard day for the freshman superstar. But the archrival Gators took a 21–20 lead on a field goal in the fourth quarter.

The Bulldogs' perfect season was in trouble. Their last chance to keep it alive began at their own 7-yard line with 90 seconds left. Their first two plays went nowhere. Then, on third down, quarterback Buck Belue scrambled to his right. He spotted wide receiver Lindsay Scott open over the middle and hit him at the Georgia 25-yard line.

But Scott wasn't satisfied with just getting a first down. Surrounded by four Florida defenders, Scott spun to his right and took off running. One Gator slipped, and that was all the opening Scott needed. With beloved radio announcer Larry Munson yelling, "Run, Lindsay, run!" Scott sprinted the final 75 yards to the end zone. The dramatic 93-yard play was Scott's only touchdown of the season, and it gave Georgia a 26–21 victory. When Notre Dame tied Georgia Tech 3–3 the same day, the Bulldogs vaulted to the top spot in the polls.

PAPER CHAMPIONS

The National Collegiate Athletic Association (NCAA) used to decide its Division I national championship on paper, not on the gridiron. Media organizations and coaching associations once conducted polls of their members to determine the national champion. Whichever team got the most votes would be declared the champion by each organization. That often led to split championships when one team didn't win each poll. In 1992 the NCAA began taking steps to ensure that the No. 1 and No. 2 teams would face off in a bowl game to determine the national title on the field.

Wide receiver Lindsay Scott races down the sideline for the game-winning touchdown against Florida.

Georgia closed out the regular season with comfortable wins over Auburn and Georgia Tech. The top-ranked Bulldogs would put their 11–0 record on the line against Notre Dame at the Sugar Bowl in New Orleans on New Year's Day.

Even though the Bulldogs were the No. 1 team in the polls, the seventh-ranked Fighting Irish were the focus of the pregame hype. After all, Notre Dame was one of the most storied programs in college football. Georgia was just another team from the SEC. That conference eventually became a powerhouse in the college football world. But in 1980, Alabama was the only SEC team that had a strong national profile.

Walker had carried the Georgia offense throughout the season. But when the Bulldogs needed him most, they nearly had to play without him. On the Bulldogs' first offensive play of the Sugar Bowl, Walker took a big hit and felt something pop.

"The doctor said I dislocated my shoulder, and they told me it was over," Walker said. "I looked at the doctor, and said, 'You've got to be joking me. You've got to put it back in place.' I told myself, 'I didn't come this far to dislocate my shoulder and not play.' So, they put it back in place, and I (went) back on the field."

But he didn't just play—he ran as he had throughout the regular season. Walker carried the ball 36 times for 150 yards on the day. He also scored both of Georgia's touchdowns.

Georgia got a big break after Robinson kicked a 46-yard field goal that made it 3–3 late in the first quarter. Notre Dame made a mistake fielding the kickoff. Both Irish returners simply let the ball fall to the Superdome turf. The Bulldogs recovered the loose ball at the 1-yard line.

Walker then jumped over the line and into the end zone. Leading 10–3, Georgia took advantage of another Notre Dame mistake early in the second quarter. Fighting Irish fullback John Sweeney fumbled deep in his own territory. The Bulldogs recovered at the 22-yard line. Walker scored on a 3-yard run three plays later to give Georgia a 17–3 lead early in that second period.

That was about all the Georgia offense could muster, but it was enough. Belue completed only one pass all day, but the two early Walker touchdowns gave the Bulldogs defense enough of a cushion. Georgia locked up the national championship with a 17–10 victory.

Walker and his teammates had all the confidence they needed when they took the 14-point lead in the second quarter. "I think we knew then

TOO SMALL?

Many experts believed that Notre Dame was going to be too big and powerful for Georgia and would be able to handle the Bulldogs easily. That did not happen, although the Irish certainly tried to win with its size and strength. But the speed of Georgia, mostly from Herschel Walker, plus the tough play of its defense changed everything around. The freshman running back proved to be too hard to stop.

"People said that we were lucky, but you're not lucky when you have people that perform," Walker said. "We were a team that was never going to quit. We were not big size-wise, but we were big at heart.

"We knew [at halftime] we had to continue to pound them with the football," he continued. "And the defense had to continue to stop them because they had such a large team. We thought they would try just to wear us down."

that we were going to win this game," Walker said. "We hadn't lost all year. We didn't know how to lose."

Walker was named Most Outstanding Player of the Sugar Bowl, capping a great freshman season on a strong note. He finished with 1,616 rushing yards and 15 touchdowns in 12 games. He'd barely played in the first half of the opening game, when his role was still uncertain. But Walker ran for two touchdowns that day at Tennessee, and he did the same thing to clinch the national title four months later in New Orleans.

[11]

A PERFECT SEASON

Sanford Stadium has been the Bulldogs' home since 1929.

THE EARLY DAYS

THE UNIVERSITY OF GEORGIA BEGAN ITS FOOTBALL PROGRAM IN THE 1892 SEASON WITH A TWO-GAME SCHEDULE. THE SCHOOL'S FIRST TEAM BEAT MERCER 50–0 AND LOST TO AUBURN 10–0

The schedule slowly expanded as time went on. In 1920 the Bulldogs had their first undefeated season with an 8–0–1 record. That year's team featured a strong defense, which posted seven shutouts and was dominant throughout the season. Herman Stegeman was the head coach that season, and he stayed for two more years. He finished with a 20–6–3 record. He also held several other positions at the school in both coaching and administration after stepping down as head coach.

The first time a Georgia team was ranked No. 1 in a national poll was in 1927. Head coach George Woodruff had played quarterback for Georgia from 1907 to 1911.

SANFORD STADIUM

Sanford Stadium, which opened in 1929, is one of the best-known stadiums not only in the SEC but in the nation. The stadium now seats 92,746 fans, making Georgia a regular among the annual attendance leaders.

The field is surrounded by a row of hedges that were planted when the stadium opened. They were inspired by the rose bushes at the Rose Bowl in Pasadena, California. Now a game at Sanford Stadium is said to have been played "between the hedges."

The school added 120,000 square feet (11,100 sq m) of new and improved space at the stadium during the 2017 season. The changes included a new home locker room, a space to host recruits on game day, a larger video board, and a new plaza that allows fans to mingle before and after games.

During that time, he also served as a team captain. As a player, Woodruff was nicknamed "Kid" because he was shorter than most of the other players. But his height did not bother W. A. Cunningham, who was the head coach at the time. Cunningham loved how tough Woodruff played despite his size.

After his time playing for the Bulldogs, Woodruff had a successful career in the insurance business in Columbus, Georgia. He also fought in World War I (1914–1918). But the pull to return to Athens was too great to resist. In 1923 Woodruff took over as the head coach at his alma mater. At the time, he was well-off financially, so he worked out an interesting contract. Woodruff agreed to be the coach for a salary of just one dollar per year.

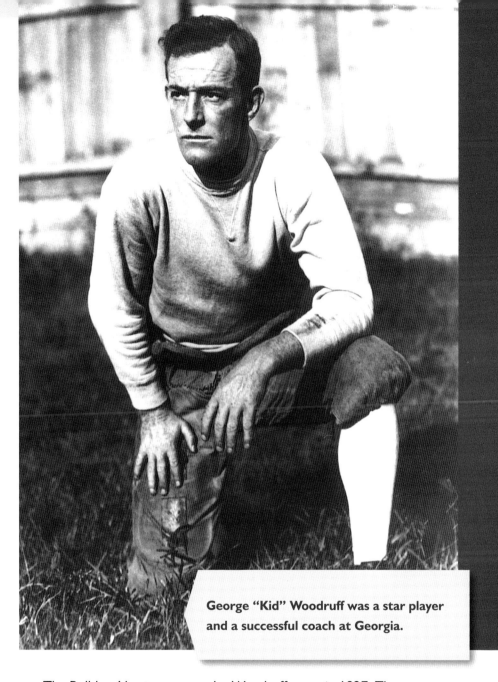

George "Kid" Woodruff was a star player and a successful coach at Georgia.

The Bulldogs' best season under Woodruff came in 1927. They won their first nine games, even beating Ivy League power Yale, one of the top college football teams of that era. Georgia was ranked No. 1 in the country with just one game left in the regular season. But Georgia Tech

spoiled any hopes of an undefeated season with a 12–0 victory. The Bulldogs ended up being picked as the No. 1 team in the nation in two recognized polls, but there was not a consensus champion.

Woodruff stepped down as the coach after that season. Sanford Stadium opened on October 12, 1929, with an overflow crowd of 30,000 on hand to watch Georgia beat Yale 15–0.

The Bulldogs were up and down after Woodruff left as coach. They posted seven winning seasons in the 1930s under head coach Harry Mehre before slipping a bit when he stepped away from the job. Then Wally Butts led a turnaround after taking over as the head coach in 1939.

In his third season, Butts led the Bulldogs to a 9–1–1 record. They earned a trip to the Orange Bowl, where the Bulldogs scored a 40–26 victory over Texas Christian University. That set everything up for the following season, when Georgia did just about everything right.

STINGY DEFENSE

The Bulldogs allowed only 17 points in 1920. That defense took a lot of pressure off the offense. Not that the offense needed much help—it scored 250 points in nine games. The only blot on the record was a scoreless tie with Virginia. That tough defense and strong offense helped the team finish 8–0–1.

That was the Bulldogs' last year as an independent. The next year, they joined the new Southern Conference. The Southern originally included six teams that now play in the SEC and six teams that are now part of the Atlantic Coast Conference. Georgia became a charter member of the SEC when it was formed in 1933.

Wally Butts was Georgia's head coach from 1939 to 1960.

3

SOUTHERN CHAMPIONS

GEORGIA'S 1942 TEAM IS REGARDED AS THE BEST IN THE FIRST 50 YEARS OF THE PROGRAM. HEAD COACH WALLY BUTTS GUIDED A POWERFUL OFFENSE THAT FEATURED HALFBACK FRANK SINKWICH, WHO WON THE HEISMAN TROPHY AS THE NATION'S BEST PLAYER THAT YEAR. THE BULLDOGS' OFFENSE FEATURED TWO OTHER ALL-AMERICANS. END GEORGE POSCHNER AND RUNNING BACK CHARLEY TRIPPI TEAMED WITH SINKWICH TO FORM A NEARLY UNSTOPPABLE ATTACK.

The Bulldogs opened the season with a 7–6 victory at Kentucky. That was the fewest points they scored in a game all season. Three more wins followed, and when the season's first national poll was taken, Georgia was ranked No. 2 in the country behind Ohio State.

Sinkwich and company kept their foot on the gas. Georgia crushed Tulane 40–0 before knocking off No. 3 Alabama 21–10 on Halloween. Ohio State lost at No. 6 Wisconsin on the same day. That vaulted the Bulldogs to the top spot in

THE FIRST

When Frank Sinkwich won the Heisman Trophy in 1942, he became the first player from the SEC to capture that honor. He set conference records that year for passing and total offense. He later went on to the National Football League (NFL) and played for two years with the Detroit Lions before an injury ended his career. After he retired, Sinkwich went on to become a successful businessman back home in Georgia.

the polls. They celebrated by stomping Florida 75–0 and Chattanooga 40–0. But then unranked and unheralded Auburn shocked the Bulldogs, pulling off a 27–13 upset.

That loss knocked Georgia back to No. 5 in the rankings. The Bulldogs were determined to rescue their national title hopes. Two days after Thanksgiving, they routed unbeaten and second-ranked Georgia Tech 34–0. The Bulldogs hoped it would be enough to earn them an invitation to play in the Rose Bowl. In those days, the Rose Bowl tried to match the best team in the country with the best team in the West. At the end of the 1942 season, Ohio State was ranked No. 1 with Georgia coming in second. But Ohio State played in the Western Conference, predecessor to the Big Ten. The Western Conference did not allow its champions to play in bowl games at that point. So Georgia got the nod to face the University of California, Los Angeles (UCLA), on January 1, 1943, in the most prestigious bowl game of them all.

UCLA came into the game ranked 13th in the nation. But the Bruins had the support of the hometown crowd on their side. The Bulldogs dominated the game statistically, outpacing UCLA 379 to 157 in yards

gained and posting 22 first downs to just four for the Bruins. But the game remained scoreless going into the fourth quarter.

Then Georgia made a big play. UCLA was pinned deep in its own territory and had to punt. Future Los Angeles Rams star Bob Waterfield tried to boot it away, but his kick was blocked. The ball bounced out of the end zone for a safety and a 2–0 Georgia lead. The Bulldogs added to that later in the quarter when Sinkwich scored on a short touchdown run. Leo Costa's kick made it 9–0. That was the final score.

The final Associated Press poll had Ohio State ranked No. 1, but six other polls put Georgia at the top. Today most observers regard the Bulldogs as the 1942 national champions. They outscored their opponents 376–76 that season and posted six shutouts that year.

SOUTHERN CHAMPIONS

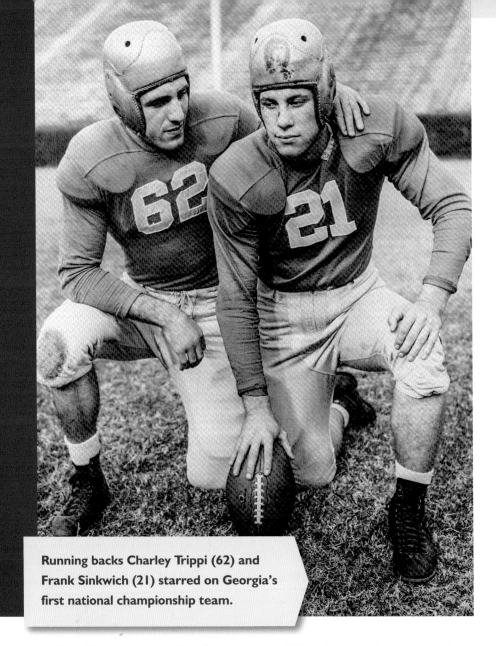

Running backs Charley Trippi (62) and Frank Sinkwich (21) starred on Georgia's first national championship team.

On offense, Sinkwich led the team with 828 rushing yards and scored 17 touchdowns. He also passed for 1,456 yards and 10 touchdowns. And he received an honor even greater than the Heisman Trophy. The Associated Press named him the top athlete in the country for 1942. He even beat out Boston Red Sox slugger Ted Williams, who had won the

That means Williams had

and runs batted in than any

still won the trophy.

three years earlier and went on

He stayed on as head coach until

0–86–9 with four SEC titles. In 2014

placed Butts No. 7 in its top 10 Georgia

ards and six touchdowns in 1942. In the Rose Bowl, he
15 yards and was named the game's Most Valuable Player
to walk off the field with a trophy. In fact, he wouldn't
another 10 years. The Rose Bowl organizers created the MVP
actively selected the winner of each game before then.
the Air Force during World War II (1939–1945). After the war,
a and won the Maxwell Award——a rival to the Heisman Trophy——in
ine seasons with the Chicago Cardinals of the NFL and is a member
all Hall of Fame and Pro Football Hall of Fame.
gia football program announced that it would give the Charley Trippi
versatile player each year.

Vince Dooley gives his players a pep talk as they prepare for the 1966 Cotton Bowl.

trip

a high

other pl

Butts ha
to have a great
1960 and compile
the *Telegraph* in Mac
coaches in any sport.

RUN AWAY

Charley Trippi rushed for 787 y
carried the ball 27 times for
(MVP). However, he didn't g
find out he was the MVP fo
Award in 1953 and retro
Trippi was drafted b
he returned to Georgi
1946. He played for n
of the College Footb
In 2012 the Geor
Award to its most

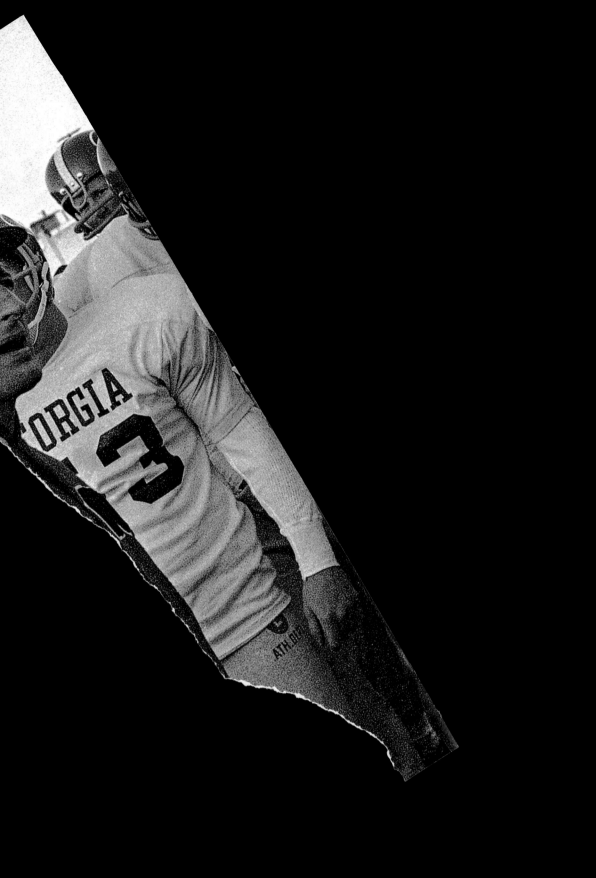

4

DOOLEY CHANGES EVERYTHING

MANY PLAYERS FROM THE 1942 NATIONAL CHAMPIONSHIP TEAM LEFT TO SERVE IN WORLD WAR II. BUT SOME OF THEM, INCLUDING CHARLEY TRIPPI, CAME BACK AFTER THE WAR AND HELPED THE TEAM GO UNDEFEATED IN 1946.

The Bulldogs were 10–0 in the regular season that year. Then they beat North Carolina in the Sugar Bowl. Georgia was the only unbeaten, untied team after the bowls were played. But Notre Dame was named the national champion by the Associated Press poll. Georgia was chosen as No. 1 in just one poll at the end of that season, and thus was not considered the national champion.

That was the closest the Bulldogs came to the national championship until Vince Dooley took over as head coach in 1964. Dooley ran the show in Athens for 25 years. His career record of 201–77–10 and that 1980 national title puts him atop the list of best coaches in Georgia history.

Uga X hangs out before a Georgia game in 2017.

Dooley was just 31 years old when he was named head coach. Over the next 25 years, he pushed the Bulldogs to another level. In 1966 they finished 10–1, won the SEC title, and beat Southern Methodist University in the Cotton Bowl. Only a regular-season loss to Miami kept them out of national championship consideration. Georgia finished ranked No. 4 that season.

The Bulldogs went 8–0–2 in the regular season in 1968, but Arkansas beat them 16–2 in the Sugar Bowl. Despite that loss, the Bulldogs were picked as the No. 1 team in the nation in one poll, but they were not considered national champions.

Georgia came close again in 1971. Sophomore quarterback Andy Johnson pushed the Bulldogs to nine straight wins before they lost to undefeated Auburn, 35–20. Still, they beat Georgia Tech in the last regular-season game and then North Carolina in the Gator Bowl, ending up 11–1. Georgia was ranked No. 6 in that season's final poll.

Five years later, Bulldogs won the SEC championship and went 10–1 in the regular season. They were ranked fifth coming into their bowl game, but they still had a chance to win the national title because they were meeting No. 1 Pittsburgh in the Sugar Bowl. However, the Panthers scored a 27–3 victory and locked up the national championship. The Bulldogs had to settle for a 10–2 record and a No. 10 ranking.

ALL ABOUT UGA

Most college sports teams have mascots. Some are more unusual than others. Some get to be very well known, like Georgia's bulldog mascot, Uga. He gets his name from the abbreviation of the school—U for University, GA for Georgia.

Uga is a white English bulldog. With his spiked collar and custom-made jerseys, Uga has been a big part of Georgia football since his debut in 1956. When he's not roaming the sidelines with his handler, Uga can be found in his air-conditioned doghouse next to the cheerleaders' platform. After each season, Uga is awarded a varsity letter, just like the athletes who contributed to the football team.

USA Today polled college football fans before the start of the 2017 season, and Uga was picked as the favorite mascot in the nation. In 2015 the football program formally introduced its 10th Uga dog, known as Uga X.

After that, Georgia slipped a bit. The Bulldogs did not make it to a bowl game in two of the next three years. They were picked as No. 16 in the preseason poll heading into the 1980 season, but Georgia was not viewed as a big threat. Then Herschel Walker burst onto the scene.

In 1980 Walker ran for 1,616 yards with 15 touchdowns despite being just a freshman. He helped lead Georgia to the national championship that year. Walker added 1,891 yards and 18 touchdowns the following year. He finished his college career with another monster season. Walker ran for 1,752 yards and 16 touchdowns in 1982. He was a shoo-in for the Heisman Trophy. In fact, he is the only player ever to finish in the top three of the Heisman voting in each year that he played.

"I've never seen a runner with such combined powers—great speed and tremendous strength, plus the intangible, burning desire to win," Dooley said. "When he won the award, I felt like a proud father. My seams were bursting. He is a very fine human being."

Walker left school with one season of eligibility remaining. He wanted to turn pro, but NFL rules didn't allow teams to sign players with any college eligibility left. So Walker tested the waters with the new United States Football League (USFL) in 1983. Walker spent three years

with the USFL's New Jersey Generals. When the league folded, he played 12 more seasons in the NFL.

Dooley, meanwhile, stayed at Georgia through the 1988 season, when he retired at the age of 56. He ended his time on the sidelines with a record of 201–77–10. His final game was a 34–27 victory over Michigan State in the Gator Bowl, played on January 1, 1989.

Georgia then quickly moved and hired a former Bulldog quarterback who was an assistant on Dooley's staff. It was a decision that did not turn out well for the program.

Ray Goff had big shoes to fill when he took over for Vince Dooley in 1989.

5

LEAN YEARS

R AY GOFF BECAME GEORGIA'S NEW HEAD COACH AFTER THE LEGENDARY VINCE DOOLEY STEPPED DOWN IN 1989. WHEN HIS HIRING WAS ANNOUNCED, EVEN THE NEW COACH HAD A BIT OF A LAUGH WITH IT.

"They've gone out on a limb, there's no doubt about it," Goff said with a chuckle.

It did not seem like that much of a risk at the time, because Goff knew Georgia football. A two-year starter at quarterback, Goff led the Bulldogs to a combined 19–5 record in 1975 and 1976. He later got into coaching and spent eight years on Dooley's staff as an assistant. He had coached the running backs for the previous three years before getting the promotion and a five-year contract at age 33. Goff knew Georgia, and Georgia knew Goff. His only problem was he could not produce wins like Dooley did.

GOING BOWLING

All-time bowl records for Georgia head coaches:

- Wally Butts (1939–60): 5–2–1
- Vince Dooley (1964–88): 8–10–2
- Ray Goff (1989–95): 2–2
- Jim Donnan (1996–2000): 4–0
- Mark Richt (2001–15): 9–5
- Bryan McClendon (2015): 1–0
- Kirby Smart (2016–): 2–1 (through 2017)

The Goff era showed signs of promise at the start. The Bulldogs made a bowl game in his first year, when they went 6–5 in the regular season before losing in the Peach Bowl. Then, after stumbling to 4–7 in 1990, they went 9–3 and 10–2 over the next two years, winning bowl games after both seasons. The 1992 squad ended the season ranked No. 8 in the Associated Press poll. It was Georgia's first top-10 finish since 1983.

But the progress stalled, and the program never found that kind of success again under Goff. Georgia followed its top-10 finish with a disappointing 5–6 season in 1993. Two six-win seasons followed, and Goff was fired as the team prepared to face Virginia in the 1995 Peach Bowl.

Jim Donnan took over for Goff and coached for the next five seasons. Donnan's Bulldogs went 40–19 overall and had winning records during each of his last four years. They also won four bowl games.

Still, the school fired Donnan just before the team was to play in the Oahu Classic after the 2000 season. The move was a bit of a surprise, as Georgia was 7–4 and ranked No. 24 in the country. Donnan's problem was that despite a strong overall record, his teams couldn't beat their

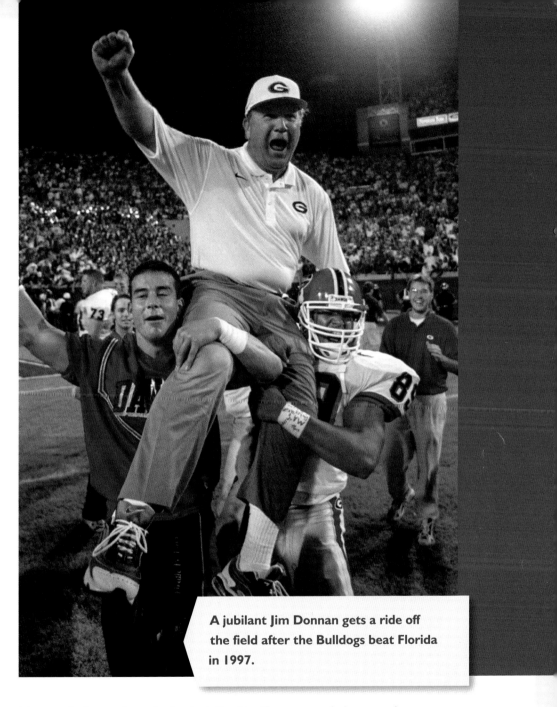

A jubilant Jim Donnan gets a ride off the field after the Bulldogs beat Florida in 1997.

biggest rivals consistently. Against Florida, Tennessee, Auburn, and Georgia Tech, Donnan's Bulldogs were 6–14. Even going 34–5 against the rest of their opponents wasn't enough to save Donnan's job.

[33]

Champ Bailey was a jack of all trades for the Bulldogs in the late 1990s.

"It's something we can't ignore," said Dooley, who was serving as the school's athletics director at the time. "Suppose we had a winning record against all four of those teams—would we be here? The fact of the matter is we would not be here if that was the case."

Donnan's best showing came in his second year as head coach, in 1997. The Bulldogs went 10–2 and throttled Wisconsin 33–6 in the Outback Bowl that year. Georgia finished 9–3 with a victory in the Peach Bowl the next year. His last two teams posted identical 8–4 records, with a win in the Outback Bowl in 1999 and the Oahu Classic in 2000 under interim coach Bryan McClendon.

Mark Richt took over as head coach after that and kept the Bulldogs as a top-level program for many years.

A LITTLE BIT OF EVERYTHING

Champ Bailey truly did it all while at Georgia from 1996 to 1998. He was a standout on both sides of the ball. While playing defensive back, Bailey intercepted eight passes in his three-year career. He became known as a "shutdown cornerback," a player who covered receivers so well that quarterbacks didn't even bother to test him.

But after concentrating on defense as a freshman, Bailey found his role in the game plan increasing. Head coach Jim Donnan looked for ways to take advantage of Bailey's athletic ability on offense, too. As a sophomore, Bailey caught 12 passes for 234 yards—an eye-popping 19.5 yards per catch. The next year, he increased his totals to 47 receptions, 744 yards, and five touchdowns. He also rushed for 99 yards over the two years.

Bailey was the seventh overall pick in the 1999 NFL Draft. He played 15 seasons with Washington and Denver. He focused almost entirely on defense and was a 12-time Pro Bowl pick at cornerback. He led the NFL with 10 interceptions in 2006.

Mark Richt and the Bulldogs celebrate an interception by Prince Miller (23) in the Sugar Bowl on January 1, 2008.

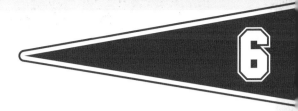

LOOKING FOR A WINNER

BY MOST ACCOUNTS, MARK RICHT HAD A SUCCESSFUL RUN AT GEORGIA. HE TOOK OVER THE PROGRAM IN 2001 AND WON 145 GAMES OVER THE NEXT 15 SEASONS. VINCE DOOLEY IS THE ONLY COACH IN PROGRAM HISTORY WHO WON MORE, WITH 201 WINS OVER 25 YEARS. RICHT ALSO WON TWO SEC CHAMPIONSHIPS, BOTH OF WHICH CAME DURING HIS FIRST FIVE YEARS.

But eventually, Richt was saddled with the reputation of a coach who couldn't win the big one. Georgia never won a national championship while Richt was the coach. Dooley won just one national title, but that championship season made him a legend in Georgia.

The closest that Richt's teams came was in 2012. The Bulldogs went 11–1 in the regular season and were ranked third in the country when they faced No. 2 Alabama in the SEC championship game. A win there would have put them in the national title game and given them a chance to win it all.

But in a hard-fought, seesaw battle, Alabama scored last and held on to win 32–28. The Crimson Tide went on to demolish Notre Dame in the Bowl Championship Series (BCS) title game. Georgia, meanwhile, had to settle for a 45–31 win over Nebraska in the Capital One Bowl. The Bulldogs ended up ranked fifth in the final polls, the high-water mark of Richt's last eight seasons in Athens.

Richt was a coach who many at Georgia loved for his personality and the way he dealt with life. He worked hard at teaching his players the right way to live their lives. He was a popular figure with his players and

TERRIFIC TANDEM

Matthew Stafford started at quarterback for Georgia from 2006 to 2008. Running back Knowshon Moreno joined him in Athens for the final two years of that span. They spent much of their time together rewriting the record books.

In 2007 the two led Georgia to the No. 2 ranking in the season-ending poll. The Bulldogs went 11–2 and hammered Hawaii 41–10 in the Sugar Bowl. Moreno rushed for 1,334 yards and 14 touchdowns, while Stafford threw 19 touchdown passes.

The next season, Stafford led the SEC with 3,459 passing yards and set a school record with 25 touchdown passes. Meanwhile, Moreno rushed for 1,400 yards and 16 touchdowns. He became the first Georgia running back since Herschel Walker to rush for at least 1,000 yards in back-to-back seasons.

The two offensive stars left Georgia to enter the 2009 NFL Draft. Stafford was the first overall choice in the draft, taken by the Detroit Lions. Moreno was selected by the Denver Broncos with the 12th pick in the first round.

Running back Knowshon Moreno (24) and quarterback Matthew Stafford had plenty of success together at Georgia.

even the school's administration. This made it a tough decision for the school to move on from such a successful, well-liked coach.

However, in 2015, Georgia director of athletics Greg McGarity and Richt agreed it was time for a change of head coach. Richt understood the situation. The Bulldogs had a 9–3 record in his final season and lost games to Alabama, Tennessee, and Florida. The Tennessee loss might

A GOOD CATCH

A. J. Green was a force at wide receiver for the Bulldogs from 2008 to 2010. He caught more than 50 passes in each of his three seasons at Georgia, and he finished with 23 career touchdowns, leading the SEC in touchdown catches in his freshman and junior seasons. He was selected by the Cincinnati Bengals with the fourth overall pick in the 2011 NFL Draft.

have been the worst because the Bulldogs blew a 21-point lead.

Richt's record at Georgia would make many schools happy. He took the Bulldogs to bowl games every year. They won at least 10 games in each of nine seasons. The Bulldogs finished second in the final Associated Press poll once, third once, and fifth once. But Richt never got them to the top spot, and that's why 15 years of winning nearly 75 percent of his games proved to be not enough.

A few weeks after Richt left, the school hired Kirby Smart as its 19th head coach. Smart had worked under Nick Saban at Alabama, most recently as the Crimson Tide's defensive coordinator. But Smart has deep local roots and important ties to the program. He grew up in Bainbridge, Georgia, and starred at defensive back for the Bulldogs from 1995 to 1998. He was a team captain during his senior year.

Smart led the Bulldogs to an 8–5 record in his first year at Georgia, closing out the season with a 31–23 win over Texas Christian in the Liberty Bowl. But his second season is one that Bulldogs fans will talk about for a long time.

Mecole Hardman scored both Georgia touchdowns in the Bulldogs' loss to Alabama in the national title game.

In 2017 Georgia was ranked as high as No. 2 in the national polls and qualified for the College Football Playoff as the third seed. Led by freshman quarterback Jake Fromm, the Bulldogs outlasted Oklahoma 54–48 in double overtime in the Rose Bowl. Then they took a 20–7 lead on Alabama in the national title game. But the Crimson Tide rallied, and Smart lost a heart-breaker to his old boss as Saban and Alabama won 26–23 in overtime.

TIMELINE

Georgia launches its football program. The Bulldogs play just two games this season, winning one and losing one.

The Bulldogs go 8–0–1 for their first undefeated season.

Georgia is voted No. 1 in one of the national polls after its "dream and wonder" team goes 9–1–0 under coach George Woodruff.

Wally Butts takes over as head coach, a job he will hold until 1960.

Frank Sinkwich wins the Heisman Trophy as Georgia finishes the regular season No. 2 in the national rankings.

1892   **1920**   **1927**   **1939**   **1942**

Georgia clinches the national championship with a 17–10 victory over Notre Dame in the Sugar Bowl on January 1. Walker is named the game's MVP.

Walker wins the Heisman Trophy in his junior year. He rushes for 1,752 yards and 16 touchdowns in his final year at Georgia.

Walker leaves Georgia after three years and signs with the new United States Football League.

Dooley steps down as the Georgia head coach, following a 25-year run.

Ray Goff takes over as head coach.

1981   **1982**   **1983**   **1988**   **1989**

The Bulldogs clinch their first consensus national championship with a 9–0 victory over UCLA in the Rose Bowl on January 1.

Charley Trippi returns from military duty and wins the Maxwell Award.

Butts steps down as head coach with a career record of 140–86–9.

Vince Dooley takes over as head coach. He will stay in charge of the program through the 1988 season, taking the Bulldogs to 20 bowl games.

Led by freshman running back Herschel Walker, the Bulldogs win the SEC and finish the regular season 11–0.

1943   1946   1960   1964   1980

Georgia lets go of Jim Donnan as head coach after five seasons.

Mark Richt takes over as the Georgia head coach.

The Bulldogs lose to Alabama in the SEC Championship game 32–28. The loss costs them a chance to play in the national title game.

Georgia lets go of Richt as head coach after 15 seasons. He is replaced by Alabama defensive coordinator Kirby Smart.

The 2017 Bulldogs go on a remarkable run before falling to Alabama 26–23 in overtime in the national title game on January 8.

2000   2001   2012   2015   2018

QUICK STATS

PROGRAM INFO*
University of Georgia Bulldogs, 1892–

NATIONAL CHAMPIONSHIPS
1942
1980

OTHER ACHIEVEMENTS
College Football Playoff appearances: 2
SEC championships: 13
Bowl record: 31–20–3

KEY PLAYERS
(POSITION, SEASONS WITH TEAM)
Champ Bailey (DB/WR, 1996–98)
Kevin Butler (K, 1981–84)
A. J. Green (WR, 2008–10)
Bob McWhorter (HB, 1910–13)
Aaron Murray (QB, 2009–13)
Jake Scott (DB, 1967–68)
Frank Sinkwich (QB, 1941–42)
Bill Stanfill (DE, 1966–68)
Fran Tarkenton (QB, 1958–60)
Charley Trippi (RB, 1942, 1945–46)
Herschel Walker (RB, 1980–82)

KEY COACHES
Wally Butts (1939–60)
  140–86–9
Vince Dooley (1964–88)
  201–77–10
Mark Richt (2001–15)
  145–51–0

HOME STADIUM
Sanford Stadium (1929–)

*statistics through 2017 season

Former Bulldogs quarterback Buck Belue said he thinks Herschel Walker is the greatest Georgia player. Belue was the quarterback for the 1980 national champions. "I don't know [that] anybody could have done that any better than Herschel did it. If those are the elements in deciding who's the greatest ever—team success, individual success, and representation—Herschel's certainly No. 1 on my list."

Uga, the Georgia mascot, has become so famous that he has a lawyer, an agent, and a professional publicist. "Yes, that's right," said Swann Seiler, who handles media relations for the dog. "It takes a village to raise a bulldog."

"Trade up for them, if you're smart."—Mark Richt, on the advice he'd give NFL teams regarding Matthew Stafford and Knowshon Moreno entering the league's draft in 2009.

"In 1959 I witnessed one of the great moments in Georgia football history when Fran Tarkenton completed a game-winning, 13-yard touchdown to Bill Herron on fourth down with just 30 seconds remaining. At the time I was an assistant coach at Auburn, the losing team, and I watched as Georgia celebrated and Sanford Stadium seemed to rock and sway and almost fall to the ground."
—Vince Dooley

GLOSSARY

All-American
Designation for players chosen as the best amateurs in the country in a particular sport.

athletics director
An administrator who oversees a university's athletics program.

conference
A group of schools that join together to create a league for their sports teams.

consensus
In college football, when all of the polls are in agreement about which team is the national champion.

draft
A system that allows teams to acquire new players coming into a league.

prestigious
Inspiring respect and admiration.

recruits
High school players targeted by colleges that want them to attend and play sports.

rival
An opponent with whom a player or team has a fierce and ongoing competition.

upset
An unexpected victory by a supposedly weaker team or player.

FOR MORE INFORMATION

ONLINE RESOURCES

Booklinks
NONFICTION NETWORK
FREE! ONLINE NONFICTION RESOURCES

To learn more about the Georgia Bulldogs, visit abdobooklinks.com. These links are routinely monitored and updated to provide the most current information available.

BOOKS

Butt, Jason. *The Georgia Bulldogs Fans' Bucket List.* Chicago, IL. Triumph Books, 2017.

Garbin, Patrick, and A. P. Garbin. *Game of My Life: Georgia Bulldogs: Memorable Stories of Bulldogs Football.* New York: Sports Publishing, 2013.

Graves, Will. *The Story of the Sugar Bowl.* Minneapolis, MN: Abdo Publishing, 2016.

PLACES TO VISIT

Sanford Stadium
100 Sanford Drive
Athens, Georgia 30602
706-542-9036
georgiadogs.com

This has been Georgia's home stadium since 1929. The stadium is named after Dr. Steadman V. Sanford, a former university president and chancellor. Check with the athletic department for information on tours for your chance to go between the hedges.

INDEX

Bailey, Champ, 35
Bates, Bill, 6
Belue, Buck, 7
Bowl Championship Series, 38
Butts, Wally, 17, 19, 23, 32

Capital One Bowl, 38
Costa, Leo, 21
Cotton Bowl, 26
Cunningham, W. A., 14

Donnan, Jim, 32–33, 35
Dooley, Vince, 5–6, 25–26, 28–29, 31, 32, 34, 37–40

Fromm, Jake, 41

Gator Bowl, 27, 29
Goff, Ray, 31–32
Green, A. J., 40

Johnson, Andy, 27

Liberty Bowl, 40

McClendon, Bryan, 32
McGarity, Greg, 39
Mehre, Harry, 17
Moreno, Knowshon, 38
Munson, Larry, 7

Oahu Classic, 35
Orange Bowl, 17
Outback Bowl, 35

Peach Bowl, 32, 35
Poschner, George, 19

Richt, Mark, 32, 35, 37
Robinson, Rex, 6, 9
Rose Bowl, 14, 20–21, 23, 41

Saban, Nick, 40–41
Scott, Lindsay, 7
Sinkwich, Frank, 19, 20, 21, 22
Smart, Kirby, 32, 40–41
Stafford, Matthew, 38
Stegeman, Herman, 13
Sugar Bowl, 8–11, 25, 26, 27, 38
Sweeney, John, 10

Trippi, Charley, 19, 23, 25

Uga, 27

Walker, Herschel, 5–6, 9–11, 28–29, 38
Waterfield, Bob, 21
Williams, Ted, 22
Woodruff, George, 13–17

ABOUT THE AUTHOR

Jeff Seidel has been a journalist in the Baltimore-Washington area for more than 30 years. He lives there with his wife, two children, and two very faithful cats.